T0022681

ASTROLOGY
SELF-CARE

Leo

♌

ASTROLOGY SELF-CARE

Leo

Live your best life by the stars

Sarah Bartlett

First published in Great Britain in 2022 by Yellow Kite
An imprint of Hodder & Stoughton
An Hachette UK company

1

Copyright © Sarah Bartlett 2022

The right of Sarah Bartlett to be identified as the Author
of the Work has been asserted by her in accordance
with the Copyright, Designs and Patents Act 1988.

Illustrations © shutterstock.com

All rights reserved. No part of this publication may be reproduced,
stored in a retrieval system, or transmitted, in any form or by any
means without the prior written permission of the publisher,
nor be otherwise circulated in any form of binding or cover
other than that in which it is published and without a similar
condition being imposed on the subsequent purchaser.

A CIP catalogue record for this title is
available from the British Library

Hardback ISBN 978 1 399 70470 0
eBook ISBN 978 1 399 70471 7
Audiobook ISBN 978 1 399 70472 4

Designed by Goldust Design

Typeset in Nocturne Serif by Hewer Text UK Ltd, Edinburgh
Printed and bound in Great Britain by Clays Ltd, Elcograf S.p.A.

Hodder & Stoughton policy is to use papers that are
natural, renewable and recyclable products and made
from wood grown in sustainable forests. The logging and
manufacturing processes are expected to conform to the
environmental regulations of the country of origin.

Yellow Kite
Hodder & Stoughton Ltd
Carmelite House
50 Victoria Embankment
London EC4Y 0DZ

www.yellowkitebooks.co.uk

*Every artist dips his brush in his own soul,
and paints his own nature into his pictures.*

Henry Ward Beecher, American
clergyman and social reformer

There is a path, hidden between the road of reason and the hedgerow of dreams, which leads to the secret garden of self-knowledge. This book will show you the way.

Contents

Introduction

The ancient Greek goddess Gaia arose from Chaos and was the personification of the Earth and all of Nature. One of the first primordial beings, along with Tartarus (the Underworld), Eros (love) and Nyx (night), as mother of all life, she is both the embodiment of all that this planet is and its spiritual caretaker.

It's hardly likely you will want to become a full-time Mother Earth, but many of us right now are caring more about our beautiful planet and all that lives upon it. To nurture and respect this amazing place we call home, and to preserve this tiny dot in the Universe, the best place to start is, well, with you.

Self-care is about respecting and honouring who you are as an individual. It's about realising that nurturing yourself is neither vanity nor a conceit, but a creative act that brings an awesome sense of awareness and a deeper connection to the Universe and all that's in it. Caring about yourself means you care about everything in the cosmos – because you are part of it.

But self-care isn't just about trekking to the gym, jogging around the park or eating the right foods. It's also about discovering who you are becoming as an individual and caring for that authenticity (and loving and caring about who we are becoming means others can love and care about us, too). This is where the art of sun-sign astrology comes in.

Astrology and Self-Care

So what is astrology? And how can it direct each of us to the right self-care pathway? Put simply, astrology is the study of the planets, sun and moon and their influence on events and people here on Earth. It is an art that has been used for thousands of years to forecast world events, military and political outcomes and, more recently, financial market trends. As such, it is an invaluable tool for understanding our own individuality and how to be true to ourselves. Although there is still dispute within astrological circles as to whether the planets actually physically affect us, there is strong evidence to show that the cycles and patterns they create in the sky have a direct mirroring effect on what happens down here on Earth and, more importantly, on each individual's personality.

Your horoscope or birth-chart is a snapshot of the planets, sun and moon in the sky at the moment you were born. This amazing picture reveals all your innate potential, characteristics and qualities. In fact, it is probably the best 'selfie' you could ever have! Astrology can not only tell you who you are, but also how best to care for that self and your own specific needs and desires as revealed by your birth-chart.

Self-care is simply time to look after yourself – to restore, inspirit and refresh and love your unique self. But it's also about understanding, accepting and being aware of your own traits – both the good and not so good – so that you can then say, 'It's ok to be me, and my intention is to become the best of myself'. In fact, by looking up to the stars and seeing how they reflect us down here on Earth, we can deepen our connection to the Universe for the good of all, too. Understanding that caring about ourselves is not selfish creates an awesome sense of self-acceptance and awareness.

So how does each of us honour the individual 'me' and find the right kind of rituals and practices to suit our personalities? Astrology sorts us out into the zodiac – an imaginary belt encircling the Earth divided into twelve sun signs; so, for example, what one sign finds relaxing, another may find a hassle or stressful. When it comes to physical fitness, adventurous Arians thrive on aerobic work, while soulful Pisceans feel nurtured by yoga. Financial reward or status would inspire the ambitious Capricorn mind, while theatrical Leos need to indulge their joy of being centre stage.

By knowing which sun sign you are and its associated characteristics, you will discover the right self-care routines and practices to suit you. And this unique and empowering book is here to help – with all the rituals and practices in these pages specifically suited to your sun-sign personality for nurturing and vitalising your mind, body and spirit.

However, self-care is not an excuse to be lazy and avoid the goings on in the rest of the world. Self-care is about taking responsibility for our choices and understanding our unique essence, so that we can engage with all aspects of ourselves and the way we interact with the world.

IN A NUTSHELL

The proud, noble and generous Lion likes to look and feel good, showing off their talents to the world. Praise and appreciation, of course, boost their self-worth, and the feeling that they are exceptional or unique. But now it's time to care more about yourself than about what other people think of you. To truly care for and nurture the Leo you – to love and inspirit self-belief and to know that you are special – follow the practices, affirmations and rituals in this book. By caring for your mind, body and spirit, you'll also discover and understand your authentic self. And what is that, if not the loving, creative and joyful Lion who spreads sunshine and happiness around wherever it goes?

Sun-Sign Astrology

Also known as your star sign or zodiac sign, your sun sign encompasses the following:

* Your solar identity, or sense of self
* What really matters to you
* Your future intentions
* Your sense of purpose
* Various qualities that manifest through your actions, goals, desires and the personal sense of being 'you'
* Your sense of being 'centred' – whether 'self-centred' (too much ego) or 'self-conscious' (too little ego); in other words, how you perceive who you are as an individual

In fact, the sun tells you how you can 'shine' best to become who you really are.

ASTROLOGY FACTS

The zodiac or sun signs are twelve 30-degree segments that create an imaginary belt around the Earth. The zodiac belt is also known as the ecliptic, which is the apparent path of the sun as it travels round the Earth during the year.

The sun or zodiac signs are further divided into four elements (Fire, Earth, Air and Water, denoting a certain energy ruling each sign), plus three modalities (qualities associated with how we interact with the world; these are known as Cardinal, Fixed and Mutable). So as a Leo, for example, you are a 'Fixed Fire' sign.

* Fire signs: Aries, Leo, Sagittarius
  They are: extrovert, passionate, assertive

* Earth signs: Taurus, Virgo, Capricorn
  They are: practical, materialistic, sensual

* Air signs: Gemini, Libra, Aquarius
  They are: communicative, innovative, inquisitive

* Water signs: Cancer, Scorpio, Pisces
  They are: emotional, intuitive, understanding

17

The modalities are based on their seasonal resonance according to the northern hemisphere.

Cardinal signs instigate and initiate ideas and projects.
They are: Aries, Cancer, Libra and Capricorn

Fixed signs resolutely build and shape ideas.
They are: Taurus, Leo, Scorpio and Aquarius

Mutable signs generate creative change and adapt ideas to reach a conclusion.
They are: Gemini, Virgo, Sagittarius and Pisces

Planetary rulers

Each zodiac sign is assigned a planet, which highlights the qualities of that sign:

Aries is ruled by Mars (fearless)
Taurus is ruled by Venus (indulgent)
Gemini is ruled by Mercury (magical)
Cancer is ruled by the moon (instinctive)
Leo is ruled by the sun (empowering)
Virgo is ruled by Mercury (informative)
Libra is ruled by Venus (compassionate)
Scorpio is ruled by Pluto (passionate)
Sagittarius is ruled by Jupiter (adventurous)
Capricorn is ruled by Saturn (disciplined)
Aquarius is ruled by Uranus (innovative)
Pisces is ruled by Neptune (imaginative)

Opposite Signs

Signs oppose one another across the zodiac (i.e. those that are 180 degrees away from each other) – for example, Leo opposes Aquarius and Taurus opposes Scorpio. We often find ourselves mysteriously attracted to our opposite signs in romantic relationships, and while the signs' traits appear to clash in this 'polarity', the essence of each is contained in the other (note, they have the same modality). Gaining insight into the characteristics of your opposite sign (which are, essentially, inherent in you) can deepen your understanding of the energetic interplay of the horoscope.

On The Cusp

Some of us are born 'on the cusp' of two signs – in other words, the day or time when the sun moved from one zodiac sign to another. If you were born at the end or beginning of the dates usually given in horoscope pages (the sun's move through one sign usually lasts approximately four weeks), you can check which sign you are by contacting a reputable site (see Resources, p. 117) who will calculate it exactly for you. For example, 23 August is the standardised changeover day for the sun to move into

Virgo and out of Leo. But every year, the time and even sometimes the day the sun changes sign can differ. So, say you were born on 23 August at five in the morning and the sun didn't move into Virgo until five in the afternoon on that day, you would be a Leo, not a Virgo.

How To Use This Book

The book is divided into three parts, each guiding you in applying self-care to different areas of your life:

* Part One: your mind and feelings
* Part Two: your body
* Part Three: your soul

Caring about the mind using rituals or ideas tailored to your sign shows you ways to unlock stress, restore focus or widen your perception. Applying the practices in Part One will connect you to your feelings and help you to acknowledge and become aware of why your emotions are as they are and how to deal with them. This sort of emotional self-care will set you up to deal with your relationships better, enhance all forms of communication and ensure you know exactly how to ask for what you want or need, and be true to your deepest desires.

A WORD ON CHAKRAS

Eastern spiritual traditions maintain that universal energy, known as 'prana' in India and 'chi' in Chinese philosophy, flows through the body, linked by seven subtle energy centres known as chakras (Sanskrit for 'wheel'). These energies are believed to revolve or spiral around and through our bodies, vibrating at different frequencies (corresponding to seven colours of the light spectrum) in an upward, vertical direction. Specific crystals are placed on the chakras to heal, harmonise, stimulate or subdue the chakras if imbalance is found.

The seven chakras are:
* The base or root (found at the base of the spine)
* The sacral (mid-belly)
* The solar plexus (between belly and chest)
* The heart (centre of chest)
* The throat (throat)
* The third eye (between the eyebrows)
* The crown (top of the head)

On p. 91 we will look in more detail at how Leos can work with chakras for self-care.

Fitness and caring for the body are different for all of us, too. While Leo benefits from dancing, for example, Taurus thrives on aromatherapy sessions and Gemini a daily quick stretch or yoga. Delve into Part Two whenever you're in need of physical restoration or a sensual makeover tailored to your sign.

Spiritual self-care opens you to your sacred self or soul. Which is why Part Three looks at how you can nurture your soul according to your astrological sun sign. It shows you how to connect to and care for your spirituality in simple ways, such as being at one with Nature or just enjoying the world around you. It will show you how to be more positive about who you are and honour your connection to the Universe. In fact, all the rituals and practices in this section will bring you joyful relating, harmonious living and a true sense of happiness.

The Key

Remember, your birth-chart or horoscope is like the key to a treasure chest containing the most precious jewels that make you you. Learn about them, and care for them well. Use this book to polish, nurture, respect and give value to the beautiful gemstones of who you are, and, in doing so, bring your potential to life. It's your right to be true to who you are, just by virtue of being born on this planet, and therefore being a child of Mother Earth and the cosmos.

Care for you, and you care for the Universe.

LEO
WORDS OF WISDOM

As you embark on your self-care journey, it's important to look at the lunar cycles and specific astrological moments throughout the year. At those
times (and, indeed, at any time you choose), the
words of Leo wisdom below will be invaluable,
empowering you with positive energy. Taking a few
mindful moments at each of the four major phases
of every lunar cycle and at the two important astrological moments in your solar year (see Glossary,
p. 119) will affirm and enhance your positive atti-
tude towards caring about yourself and the world.

NEW CRESCENT MOON – to care for yourself:

'Although I put myself first, I will always be loyal to true friends.'

'The person I am becoming is the best part of myself and reveals my true potential.'

'Character is who I am, reputation is what others think I am.'

FULL MOON – for sealing your intention to care for your feeling world:

'I will make an effort to care for my inner self, and not worry so much about my image and how to live up to it.'

'Tell me and I may not remember, show me and I may not keep up, involve me and I will be there and will understand.'

'In my tranquillity, I am happy, healthy and fulfilled.'

WANING MOON – for letting go, and letting things be:

'I need to stop avoiding the truth, and let others have their own.'

'By learning I will teach; by teaching I will learn.'

'The beauty of this planet weaves through me too; I relinquish all fear of being imperfect.'

DARK OF THE MOON – to acknowledge your 'shadow' side:

'I need to overcome my reluctance to admit failure. I must acknowledge my feelings, and most of all not expect so much of others.'

'If I come from a place of peace within myself, I will discover peace all around me.'

'I can make mistakes with pride because every error is a learning experience.'

SOLAR RETURN SALUTATION – welcoming the sun's return to your own sign, to be true to who you are:

Repeat on your birthday: 'All the world's a stage, and all the men and women merely players, but as a Leo I want the stage to myself. There are times when I will be in the limelight, but must accept that others will be, too.'

SUN IN OPPOSITION – learn to be open to the opposite perspective that lies within you.

Repeat when the sun is in Aquarius: 'My opposite sign is Aquarius who gives to the world all that it needs and asks nothing in return. This sign is in my birth chart, too, so I must give thanks to the care that I can show humanity.'

The Leo
Personality

♌

*Keep your face to the sunshine
and you cannot see the shadows.*
Helen Keller, author

Characteristics: Charismatic, warm-hearted,
dignified, dramatic, proud, stylish, romantic,
opinionated, self-important, creative, artistic,
self-focused, loyal, luxury-loving, confident,
ambitious, regal, imaginative, theatrical,
status-seeking

Symbol: the Lion
In Greek mythology, Leo was identified with the
ferocious Nemean lion whose golden mane and fur
shielded him from warriors or attack. The lion was
eventually killed by Heracles, and Zeus honoured
him by placing him in the sky.

Planetary ruler: the Sun

The centre of our 'solar system', the sun is a constantly changing star, and one day it will become a red giant. In approximately 5 billion years, it will have grown large enough to engulf the orbits of Mercury and Venus and the Earth will be uninhabitable. The sun will then slowly cool down to become a white dwarf.

Astrological sun: Representing the solar centre of oneself, the sun also reveals our purpose, will and meaning in life. Depending on its relation to other planets in the chart, it can also signify how aware – or not – we are of these potentials.

Element: Fire

Like the other Fire signs, Sagittarius and Aries, Leo is concerned with the ideas, beliefs, ideals, imagination and creativity of life, rather than its practicalities.

Modality: Fixed

'Fixed' means being sure of one's purpose, but also unwilling to bend from it. This tenacity manifests in Leos' opinions and belief that they know more and better than anyone else. Fixed signs follow the rules – as long as they're rules they've set for themselves. Leos use this single-mindedness to prove they're special.

Body: In astrology, each sign rules various parts of the body. Leo traditionally rules the heart and spine.

Crystal: Sunstone

Sun-sign profile: Sun-ruled Leos love to shine and bring the world to life, too. This idealistic, charismatic Fire sign wants to be centre stage, and their theatrical flamboyance is a means to feeling appreciated and worthy. As long as the Lion has an adoring entourage or audience, they are the most exciting and loving of signs. Theatre and glamour are Leo's proud friends, but beneath the flashy exterior, the Lion has a soft heart, and is one of the most generous, loyal and giving of souls. Leos believe they deserve the best because they simply are the best. They expect the rest of the world to take care of them, no matter what. When these fiery desires are directed into creative pursuits it reinforces the Lion's sense of self-esteem, and the roaring cat's dependence on the love of others switches to showing their love for them instead.

Your best-kept secret: Behind that dramatic, glitzy exterior is a vulnerable child who lives in a fairytale world. You will never give up the idea of living a theatrical life for anything or anyone else.

What gives you meaning and purpose in life?
Showing off your talents, being praised, being centre
stage, getting your way, being in love, becoming
famous or highly successful

What makes you feel good to be you? Having
admirers, not having rivals, being pampered, love,
sex and champagne, proving a point

What or who do you identify with? Celebrities,
film stars, VIPs, leaders, royalty, luxury items,
the best restaurants, the stage, theatre, famous artists

What stresses you out? Not being admired, failing
to get a round of applause, giving someone a
present and not getting anything back, feeling
invisible, having to prove something or live up to
your claims

What relaxes you? Pampering yourself, shopping for
luxury items, indulging in favourite foods and guilty
pleasures; a busy social life where you are number one

What challenges you? A partner who doesn't 'read
your mind', people who don't live up to your high
expectations, your own imperfections, being only
human

What Does Self-Care Mean For Leo?

The world really does revolve around the iconic big cat, and Leos have little trouble caring about their image and reputation. In fact, the way you dress, the way you do your hair and any form of beauty ritual are firmly under your control. You know how to play the perfect role on stage, put on a grand performance, steal the spotlight from others, bask in the glory of fame and success or achieve an ambition. All these things nurture and nourish your fiery, individualistic spirit. But how do you care for yourself in ways other than just preening your glamorous facade?

Self-care for you includes expressing the divine spark within to showcase your creative talents – receiving the recognition you deserve because of those gifts, not just because you have charmed others into singing your praises.

Self-Care Focus

The Leo self-care practices in this book will inspire you to unleash your creativity, be sunshine personi-fied, influence others and be charismatic and desirable. You need to do something unique and flamboyant in the big, wide world to maximise your self-value. So if you're not literally acting on a stage, running your own business or painting a masterpiece, then you are destined to create some kind of theatre in your life on a smaller scale. It's not about changing who you are, but about living out your potential and embracing the qualities that make you that person. Self-care for you, Leo, is about nurturing and expressing the sacred creativity within you, to give you a genuine sense of self-worth.

PART ONE

Caring For Your Mind And Feelings

Your children are not truly your children. They are the sons and daughters of life's yearning for itself.

Kahlil Gibran, writer and poet

This section will inspire you to delight in your thoughts, express your ideas and take pleasure in your feelings. Once you get that deep sense of awareness of who you are and what you need, not only will it feel good to be alive, but you will be even more content to be yourself. The rituals and practices here will boost your self-esteem, motivate you to lead a more serene existence and enhance all forms of relationships with others. The most important relationship of all, with yourself, will be nurtured in the best possible way according to your sun sign.

Would you love to live a mythical life or an ordinary one? I think you'd probably go for the first. In fact, many Lions somehow manage to fabricate fascinating stories or create mystique and intrigue around themselves. If you're not inventing a drama or lifestyle where you rise like a flame above all the drabness and dullness of ordinary life, then get started now. You thrive on having something theatrical going on in your life so you can shine brighter than anyone else. All the arts – film, TV, fine art, sculpture and so on – provide you with a medium for expressing your flair for drama and crisis. You're also a brilliant editor because you creatively cut out the boring, leaving something memorable in its place. All of this involves being a little mysterious and outrageous, generating curiosity and awe in others. So your fabulous stories, whether invented, true or over-dramatised for the sake of a reaction, are all brilliant manifestations of your creative mind.

Here are some ways to inspire and vitalise that creativity, to love yourself for being that roaring mythical beast of the constellations, connect you to your feeling world and create the success you deserve.

Daily Inspiration

Apart from your usual beauty and body rituals, here are a few tips for getting the day off to a good start. I know you don't like other people telling you what to do, so this is not set in stone, but intentionally dedicate at least, say, five minutes each day to one or all of the following to inspire you:

SCRIBING

I've used the word 'scribing' here instead of 'journaling' because it sounds more in keeping with Leo's theatre of life. It enables you to act like a privileged ancient Egyptian scribe who wrote mysterious messages on walls, temples, tombs and papyrus. You can tell your friends about how you 'scribe' every day, and discover truths hidden within you!

You can use a diary, a journal or a beautiful sketchbook (then you can doodle and stick things in it, too).

As you begin, imagine yourself seated in a pharaoh's palace, your pen made from finest reed, the papyrus still exuding the odour of wetland sedge. You may want to get your thoughts down, clear your mind of anything that bothers you, along with whatever fascinates or motivates you. Don't feel you have to write down facts or lists; you could simply write romantic nonsense or poetry for the pleasure of it. But whatever you write, make it a grand gesture for yourself, in keeping with the scribe's prestigious profile.

SCRIBBLING

To nurture your artistic side, do a little scribbling before you go out in the morning, whether with paint or pencil. Scribble painting is simply making a variety of random, abstract marks across a piece of paper or canvas without regard for composition or form. When you return to it later, you can admire your work, tear it up or plan to develop it. The great joy is that you've expressed something already on paper before you even start the day.

SANCTUARY

Create a place in your home specifically for self-care. Here you can sit and sip your morning tea, write or do some simple visualisations or mindful relaxation. Perhaps place some crystals, flowers or candles to inspire and nurture good feelings. This is a place of beautiful intentions, so keep it free of daily clutter or jumbled thoughts. It is somewhere you can sit and listen to the silence (no radios, phones, computers, emails or TV). You can use it as your space for your daily scribble and scribe (as above) or for some of the other rituals in this book. It may be that you only sit here for one minute, but the energy of this space will care for you.

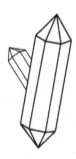

OUROBOROS FUN

The Lion is very aware of how special they are, but Leos need to remind themselves of who exactly that individual is, among all the roles they play out there on the world stage. The ancient symbol of the snake eating its own tail, known as the ouroboros, is an iconic motif for the unity of the self and for confirming one's individuality.

You will need:
* An image of the ouroboros (any size you like) or paints and paper
* A pen

1. Paint, draw or cut out an image of an ouroboros.

2. Write your name over and over again around the outside of the snake to form a circle around it.

3. Inside the snake's coil, write the words 'All is one, all is one', as many times as you can fit them, spiralling them out from the centre, until the whole of the interior of the snake circle is covered with these words.

Place the ouroboros image in your home where you'll see or pass by it every day – say, a hallway, entrance or bedroom – to empower you with self-belief. The sense of 'oneness' you will gain will be a daily reminder that the many different roles you play on your world stage actually make up the 'one' you.

SIMPLY THE BEST

Your greatest role models for self-care are the sun god Apollo and the zodiac Lion. The Lion, of course, is proud, magnificent, self-important and yet socially engaging (with his own clan, at least). Apollo, the god of light, sun, music, prophecy, knowledge and beauty, embodies all of Leo's graciousness and creative power . Here's how to incorporate their respective qualities into your life and reaffirm your Leo power.

You will need:
* A mirror
* 2 gold candles
* 2 60 cm (24 inch) lengths of gold thread, string or twine

1. Sit before the mirror and place a candle either side of it.

2. Form a circle around each candle with the gold threads to seal your intention for Apollo's will and the Lion's magnanimity.

3. Light the candles and gaze into the mirror.

4. Focus for a few minutes on the flames' reflections, rather than yourself, then look yourself straight in the eye in the mirror and say: 'I am blessed with the golden heart of the Lion and the divine gold of Apollo. I am now ready to shine brightly wherever I go.'

This practice will help you to be simply the best of you, especially when you need to shine brighter than anyone else.

LUXURY PERSONIFIED

Leos are renowned for expressing their glamorous allure by wearing ostentatious clothes and accessories such as costume jewellery, billowing scarves or fabulous hats.

The Leo signature, if not expressed, can lead you to becoming an invisible or miserable Lion. So if you can't afford the luxury items you crave (unless you're one of those Leos who enjoys rummaging through charity shops), follow this visualisation ritual to boost your sense of pageantry. It is your right to embellish yourself like a queen bee and maintain that dignified, flamboyant aura.

1. Visualise a giant treasure chest made of ornate gold on the table before you.

2. As you open it, see that it is like a bottomless well, filled with antique jewels, gemstones, bracelets, rings – a treasury of luxurious delights.

3. Reach in and pull out a ruby on a gold chain. Beneath it are gold embroidered taffeta shoes, a fine silk dress and a tiara that must sit on some princess's head.

4. Take out each gift with care, mentally adorning and dressing yourself with as many of these luxuries as you imagine. The chest holds endless treasures – all gifts to you.

5. See yourself wearing these riches and living the luxury status you so desire.

6. Close the treasure chest and come out of your visualisation.

Hold the images from this practice with you as you go about your daily business; imagine yourself in the role of treasure seeker and how you have also found the true motifs of being special. See the jewels that adorn your hair or body as simply manifestations of your own inner gems, and how your stylish allure inspires the world around you.

MANIFEST MAGNIFICENCE

As a larger-than-life divine child, it's hardly surprising you desire a magnificent lifestyle. It may not be possible to live in Hollywood or own an island, but you can at least imagine yourself up there with the most iconic people in the world. As they say, 'What goes around, comes around, and sometimes tenfold'.

The art of manifestation is to put out so much belief or desire that the Universe will oblige. If you are constantly moaning, the Universe will moan back at you. So do this simple ritual to ensure you get what you most want. If you really and truly believe it, the Universe will put its belief in you, too.

You will need:

* An image of a role model, a place or anything representing the life you are seeking
* A favourite book – one you will never throw out or recycle!

1. Think long and hard about what 'magnificence' means to you, and how you can relate this to a practical and possible lifestyle.

2. Now write on the back of your image, in as few words as possible, what you desire.

3. Place the image randomly inside the book and put it in a safe place: a bookshelf, your study, under your bed – somewhere secret or where you won't lose it.

4. Now petition this desire to the Universe by saying aloud: 'With this written intention I seek the magnificent lifestyle I choose; please help me to realise my dream.'

If you continue to visualise the kind of life you truly desire and sincerely believe it will come true, the Universe will oblige.

CRYSTAL MAGIC

Feeling that you are special or being singled out for a leading role on the world's stage is all very well, but if other people aren't giving you the attention you feel you deserve, your roaring Lion becomes a frustrated or needy one. To restore, balance and reclaim your power, perform this ritual at every full moon. Gold is Leo's magical colour, and as the fifth sign of the zodiac, five is your special number of creativity, luck and success.

You will need:
* 5 gold tea lights
* 5 crystals: sunstone, goldstone, amber, tiger's eye, citrine

1. Put the candles in a horizontal row on a table in front of you.

2. Place a crystal in front of each tea light and then light the wicks.

3. Focus on the first flame.

4. Pick up the crystal in front of this flame and hold it tightly in your fist for thirty seconds.

5. Replace the crystal and say: 'With this gold stone I reclaim my power'.

6. Repeat with each of the remaining flames and crystals.

In a very short time, you will feel that sense of being special again.

LEARN TO LAUGH

'The Fool' is the tarot card with no number. He is reckless, exciting, a bit of a show-off and doesn't care much about anyone else (unless they are praising him), preferring the open road to the cul de sac. But although he often laughs at the world, he is also capable of laughing at himself. Like the Fool, take time to be amused by you – because laughing *at* yourself means you're laughing *with* yourself.

You will need:
* A Fool tarot card (or, if you don't have a deck of tarot cards, a printout or a sketch or a painting of the Fool will do)
* A sunstone or tiger's-eye crystal

1. Place your card or image on a window ledge on a full-moon evening.

2. Place your sunstone or tiger's eye on top of the image and leave for twenty-four hours to reinforce your crystal with the laughter of the Fool and the power of sun and moon.

Take your laughing 'Fool' crystal with you when you're out walking or 'performing' on your chosen stage, and the magic of laughing at and with yourself will bring you creative inspiration and the perfect performance.

SHARING THE SPOTLIGHT

It's not easy for Leo to share the stage, except with someone who's playing a minor role. The following visualisation will help you to accept that others might deserve a share of the limelight, too.

1. Imagine an opera being performed. The huge cast are singing bel canto and two divas are waiting in the wings to come on stage for their duet. You are one of these divas.

2. As you glide into the limelight, your 'rival' diva glides next to you. The audience oohs and ahhs at your beauty, your brilliant soprano voices. Then they clap and applaud you both as you finish the duet.

3. You turn to look at your rival and she's smiling at you, and clapping, too. Be aware of her praise of you; see it as praise given to all divas, and then humbly accept that you are just one of them. Treasure the praise you now give to her, and the applause she receives from the audience. By clapping your hands to respect her talent, you are praising all divas, including yourself.

Practising this visualisation will put an end to any resentment or feelings of being threatened by someone else's presence.

....

RUNES FOR SELF-EMPOWERMENT

Runes are a form of secret writing used by ancient Norse and Germanic tribes. The mysterious symbols are best known for being carved on standing stones throughout Scandinavia. Inscribed on talismans and charms, too, they were thought to resonate with the universal wisdom of time past, present and future. Each rune represents a quality to treasure.

Self-empowerment is about feeling magical, magnificent and dignified, but also serene, stylish and privileged. Use these specific runes to enhance your best qualities.

You will need:
* An image of Dagaz – the rune of awakening, sunrise, realisation
* An image of Sowilo – the rune of vitality, will, the sun, intention, success
* 2 scraps of paper
* A pen or pencil

1. Copy each image on to a scrap of paper.

2. On a full-moon night, fold up the two scraps and place them under your pillow to attract their associated qualities to you.

Keep these scraps of paper on your person or in your bag the next day and you will be blessed with style and distinction.

....

CAT RITUAL

You know you're a big cat, the greatest lion of all lions; but there's a little pussycat of the domestic variety within you, too. Nocturnal, enigmatic, stealthy and clever with its claws, the domestic cat has been revered since ancient Egyptian times.

Leo is associated traditionally with certain crystals that, due to their structure, create an effect known as 'chatoyancy', derived from the French term *oeil de chat*, meaning cat's eye. These crystals include tiger's eye and chrysoberyl (also known as cat's eye, just to confuse things).

Harness the crystal quality of chatoyancy with your own cat-like self, using the practice below.

You will need:
* A tiger's eye
* A moonstone
* A red candle

1. Place the two stones on a table either side of the red candle.

2. Light the candle.

3. Pick up the tiger's eye and hold it in your hand. Gaze into the stone and focus on your greatest strengths, such as your charisma, the way you are special and unique. Keep the tiger's eye in your hand.

4. Next, take up the moonstone in your other hand. Gaze into it and focus on your weaknesses, your lack of true self-value and the kitten inside who is always trying to compensate by flexing her claws into a ball of wool to prove something.

5. Come out of your focus and replace the stones.

6. As you blow out the candle, feel gratitude for your big cat and care for your domestic kitten, now that they have both found you.

This practice will unleash your Leonine confidence, along with a peppering of self-esteem and nurturing for the domestic kitten within.

FORGIVENESS

In ancient Greek mythology, Eos was the goddess of the dawn. Rosy-fingered she scattered dew across the grass and, at the moment of sunrise, she lit the world with her golden glow. However, Eos was put under a curse by the jealous Aphrodite, who gave her an unquenchable desire for beautiful, young, mortal men.

One myth tells of how Eos fell for Prince Tithonus and asked Zeus to grant him eternal life. However, Eos forgot to ask for eternal youth, too, and as Tithonus aged, he shrivelled and shrank. No longer beautiful, he frizzled up like a piece of burnt bacon, but because Eos regretted her mistake, the gods pitied him and turned him into a cicada.

Consider how this myth relates to you. Well, out there, in the big, wide world, you, like Eos, search for an ideal – a perfect partner, a perfect you – yet something always comes along to pull the rug out from under you. Maybe the partner or the job aren't as you thought they would be. Or perhaps you can't live up to your own ideal of love or of the success you have created for yourself. Like Eos, perhaps you have to live with the fact that no one is perfect, not even you. But remember that the

63

gods forgave her, and the cicada chirps merrily in the trees. And realise that you don't have to regret your choices – just forgive yourself a little and accept who you are.

Relationships

With childlike enthusiasm, the 'sun king' or 'queen bee' has high expectations of romantic relationships, fanning the flames of idealistic love for as long as possible. To you, love should be like an Arthurian legend with knights in shining armour and scenes of courtly love. And if an affair doesn't create a magnificent showcase for you, you'll move on to another lover who will put you on a pedestal. However, once committed, you give everything to the one you love, demanding complete loyalty in return. Being so dependent on the love of others for a sense of self-worth means you'll do anything in your seductive power to be loved.

One myth that resonates with Leo's relationship style is that of Apollo and Cassandra. In an attempt to seduce the princess of Troy, the sun god Apollo gave Cassandra the gift of prophecy. Cassandra took the gift but didn't fall for Apollo's charms. In revenge, Apollo (not all goodness and light when physical desire was at stake) put a curse on her that nobody would ever believe what she said, even though her prophecies were always right.

Like Apollo, you too must learn that if someone receives your gift but doesn't give you back what you expect, maybe it says more about your assumptions than their lack of passion.

PERFECT LOVE

The Lion often has an idealistic vision of love and may need to be a little more realistic about their relationship goals. To understand how impractical or over-romanticised your goals are, paint a picture or visualise how you see your love paradise:

1. Where would you reside with your lover? On a sun-drenched beach? In a chateau surrounded by golden fields? On a millionaire's yacht?

2. Next, ask yourself how realistic this picture is. Do you have to come down to Earth a little, and lower your expectations of people and especially of yourself?

3. Now write down, paint or compose lyrics about what you want from a relationship. As you do so, ask yourself whether you want physical fun, mutual adoration, to be looked after, to be pampered . . . Is it just that you want to be the star of the show, and be constantly told that you're special? Do you want to be part of a couple or would you like to maintain your independence?

4. Keep your painting or ramblings safe and refer to them whenever you feel as if life or love aren't giving you back what you had hoped for. It will give you a reality check and help you to realise you may be asking for too much.

....

WHO CAN YOU TRUST?

You have a tendency to trust others too easily. One reason for this is that you want to see the best in everyone; another is that it's actually such a waste of time checking up on people and their motives, when you could be having fun.

This simple candle ritual will reveal who you can and can't trust with your heart, secrets or ideas. To maximise the available energy to work in your favour, perform this during the dark of the moon – the time just before the new crescent moon.

You will need:

* Some tea lights (one for each of the people you want to check up on)
* A pin

1. Place your tea lights on a firm, flat surface, spaced well apart.

2. Remove a tea light from its metal casing and use the pin to etch into the side of the candle the name of someone you want to psych out.

3. Return the tea light to its metal casing (for safety) and light it.

4. Blow gently across the flame with each out-breath, waiting and watching how the flame moves for a minute or so. If the flame stays very still and true, then this person is, likewise, honest and true. If the flame dances a little, then settles down, then this person cannot keep secrets, but is basically honest. If the flame goes out or constantly flickers, you should not trust this person.

5. Repeat with the remaining candles/people, blowing out each one before moving on to the next.

Keep the 'trusted' candles in a safe place for one lunar cycle; discard the 'untrustworthy' ones, making a note of the people in question.

....

INVOKING LOYALTY

In Eastern traditions, the tiger lily is said to represent compassion and nurturing, while the rose is associated with romance and happiness. The two flowers together represent the power of love and loyalty.

As a Leo, you require utter commitment and loyalty once you've found 'the one'. Anything less than twenty-four/seven dedication from your partner can seem like a kind of betrayal. Do this simple ritual during a new crescent-moon phase to nurture feelings of loyalty.

You will need:

* 2 tiger lilies
* A yellow ribbon
* 2 red or pink roses
* A red or pink ribbon
* Ylang-ylang essential oil
* A vase

1. Bind the two tiger-lily stems together with the yellow ribbon.

2. Bind the two rose stems together with the red or pink ribbon.

3. Sprinkle the flowers with a few drops of the ylang-ylang essential oil.

4. Place the flowers in the vase and keep it in a room where you will see it frequently during the day.

This symbolic gesture will invoke loyalty, restore faith in yourself and others and nourish your inner self.

PART TWO

Caring For Your Body

If anything is sacred, the human body is sacred.

Walt Whitman, poet

Here, you will discover alternative ways to look after and nurture your body, not just as a physical presence, but its connection to mind and spirit, too. This section gives you a wide range of ideas, from using sun-sign crystals to protect your physical and psychic self to fitness, diet and beauty tips. There are specific chakra practices and yoga poses especially suited to your sun sign, not forgetting bath-time rituals and calming practices to destress and nurture holistic wellbeing.

Your ruling planet, the sun, is associated with the heart and spine. With an intuitive awareness of what is physically good for you, you quickly choose self-care practices that you know will benefit fitness, looks and physique.

As nothing is more inspiring or exciting for you than people clamouring for your attention, get on the dance floor or down the gym where you can cause a stir with your perfectly toned physique and graceful movements. Salsa or Latino rhythms are great for flexing those well-groomed limbs and toning up your muscles, while aerobic exercise such as brisk walks or jogging relax you, support your heart and circulation and cool your stress levels. Here are some other ways to get your body beautiful into glorious shape.

Fitness and Movement

High-energy workouts are great for aerobic exercise, but gentler forms can be just as effective and help you to stretch, calm your mindset and release any negativity. Choose a Pilates, yoga or dance class and indulge in the admiration and acclaim you receive from your classmates. This kind of self-gratification is beneficial to you personally, so don't listen to those who try to tell you otherwise. Simply remind yourself that you want the best because you believe you deserve it.

THE CALM – BEACH VISUALISATION

You can't always be superwoman but not achieving your best usually stresses you out. So to calm yourself, try this simple visualisation:

1. Take a few long, deep breaths.

2. Imagine you are lying on the most beautiful white beach in glorious sunlight. You can hear the waves gently and slowly lapping rhythmically on the shore. As you listen to them, you hear your in-breaths and out-breaths, too, synchronised with the lapping waves.

3. As your breathing slows and deepens, and as the sounds of the calming waves diminish, you will begin to relax and feel restored again.

Use this practice whenever you feel a little overwhelmed by life and need to feel like a purring pussycat again.

DANCE WITH NATURE

The early-twentieth-century American dancer Isadora Duncan believed dance to be a sacred art. Considered to be the 'mother' of modern dance, she developed her own unique free dance style, based on classical Greek arts. In ancient Greek mythology, it was believed nymphs skipped and leaped across the mountainside to keep the Nature gods amused and thus promote the fertility of the land.

Leos are born dancers, with an innate affinity for artistic movement and rhythm and, of course, for expressing the emotions behind the music or choreography. If you're not already into classical ballet, waltzes, tangos, jives or more contemporary styles, dancing is a superb way to nurture your physical grace and artistic self-expression and show off your natural joie de vivre. So why not try some of this natural free movement, with no steps to follow, except your own?

Go out to a place you like in Nature – a wood, a riverbank, a park, a hill, a beach, whatever takes your fancy. Imagine the music in your head and twirl, pirouette, leap, skip or place your arms around a make-believe partner. Liberate your senses and enjoy the improvised dance you are creating. Then, when you have had enough, relax, knowing that your dancing keeps you physically fit, graceful and supple, as well as being a magical expression of who you are. And maybe you have amused the Nature gods, too?

Nutrition

Like any hungry lion, Leos will gorge themselves at a feast, eat everything on their plates and often overindulge in all the little extravagances of food and drink. Eating smaller servings of favourite foods, including a good, varied diet of fruit and vegetables, will help to balance your nutritional health. Eating three large meals a day may be tempting, but little and often will do more to support Leo's fiery nervous system and the need to be on the go all day.

SUNFLOWER HEALTH

Leo's ruling planet, the sun, is associated with both the heart and the sunflower. The seeds of this magnificent flower are rich in vitamin E, known for its ability to regulate cholesterol levels and support heart health – the key to your Leo physical health profile.

Try to include sunflower seeds or sunflower-seed oil in your daily diet. One way to enjoy this sun-loving plant's beneficial seeds is by using sunflower-seed butter. You can spread it on toast or pancakes or use in sandwich fillings. Here's a simple way to incorporate it into your busy Leo day.

You will need:
* Porridge or oats (1 serving)
* Natural yoghurt (dairy or dairy-free, as preferred)
* Sunflower-seed butter

1. Prepare your bowl of porridge or oats, according to taste.

2. Mix in the yoghurt, then drizzle over or stir in the sunflower seed butter.

This delicious, quick and nutritious breakfast will provide a balanced and beneficial start to the day ahead and help to maintain your fiery Leo energy levels.

COFFEE BREAK

♡

If you want to turn heads, then next time you're taking a break from work, here's a delicious way to entertain your fans and enjoy a nutritional indulgence at the same time.

What's more attention-grabbing than walking into a room sipping a huge cappuccino, topped with froth, mounds of whipped cream, a squirt of caramel and a sprinkling of chocolate shards? Or invent your own recipe. You deserve to indulge in your favourite things whenever you get the urge – it means you are being true to your Leo nature. It might be that you have to ask the local cafe to prepare something that's not on their menu; but you may well be doing them a favour, too, giving them a new creative idea to chalk up on their board?

Beauty

Leo loves to devote a lot of time to make-up, beauty routines and choosing the right clothes and accessories for any occasion. Even as children, Leos dress up in theatrical costumes, adorn themselves in fantasy jewellery and stagger around their homes in their mothers' high heels. So if you're not already totally dedicated to the way you look, now's the time to really strut your stuff and receive the compliments you deserve.

MANE EVENT

Show off your hair! In most cultures worldwide, hair has been either a symbol of strength and virility or of mystique, seduction and status. In ancient Greece, long, thick black hair was a sign of feminine wiles and magic, while in nineteenth-century Europe, golden or blonde hair was associated with beauty and wealth.

Whether you tame your locks or let them grow wild, your hair shows off your Leo majesty to the world. Here's a simple natural beauty tip to give your hair a magical glow and enchant all around you.

You will need:

* 2 tbsp almond or olive oil

1. Apply the oil in sections to your scalp.

2. Massage with gentle circular motions, increasing the pressure as required over the entire scalp.

3. Leave the oil in your hair overnight for best results, and shampoo and rinse the next morning.

Your luxuriant hair will be the crowning glory of your next stage performance.

....

SUN – BATHING RELAXATION GESTURE

Although you rarely sit down for long, there are times when the big cat wants to purr, not roar, and there's nothing Leo likes better than sun-bathing. So when you fancy flopping on to the nearest lounger to bask in the heat and tan your skin, perform this simple mudra (a Hindu hand gesture) to fire your spirit with solar energy, too.

1. As you lie there in the sun, place your hands in front of your belly button, fingers interlaced with little fingers pointing up to form an inverted V.

2. Stay like this for a peaceful five minutes and visualise the letter V in your mind.

Enjoy the sun! Your skin will be enriched with vitamin D, and you with the V of a victorious self-caress.

....

A GIRL'S BEST FRIEND

Another form of bathing that does Leo the world of good is in the bathtub. (If you don't have a bath, you can adapt this practice for a shower.)

You will need:
* 4 gold tea lights
* 4 tiger's-eye crystals
* Bubble bath of your choice
* Rose essential oil
* A rough uncut diamond (they're not cheap – but you're worth it, aren't you?) or a small clear quartz crystal

1. Place the four candles and the four tiger's eye crystals at each corner of the bath.

2. Light the candles.

3. Fill your bath, adding your chosen bubble bath.

4. Add 3 drops of rose essential oil to the water.

5. Place your 'diamond' in the bath with you, in between your feet. Relax and see the diamond as your 'best friend', to inspire you with superb ideas in the days to come.

This bathing ritual will make you feel pampered and inspired with brilliance.

CHAKRA BALANCE

The body's chakras are the epicentres of the life-force energy that flows through all things (see p. 22).

Leo is associated with the crown chakra, which is the channel for the inward flow of wisdom. Located on the top of the head, it is where you receive the gift of cosmic connection. And let's not forget, it's also where your wonderful mane of shining locks is situated.

If the crown chakra is underactive, you will feel frustrated and concerned about making a good impression, always worrying about what other people think of you. You may panic because you weren't contacted immediately after that amazing job interview or freak out because your latest date hasn't texted you yet – and you've only just got in the taxi to go home! To restore balance to this chakra, wear or carry clear quartz crystal to enhance willpower and improve self-belief and self-confidence in all you do.

If the crown chakra is overactive, you may think you're some kind of guru or celebrity, talk about yourself non-stop and not care about anyone else's feelings. You expect everyone to come running when you click your fingers or walk around with your nose in the air. To subdue this overactive chakra and enable you to get your head back down to earth and out of the clouds, wear or carry an opal – this calms emotions and enhances clear thinking.

General Wellbeing

Whether at home or out there in your social world, as a Leo you need to feel not only in control of your appearance, but also protected and empowered, so you can truly shine your light in the best possible way. Here are some simple ideas to bring you a sense of wellbeing and security, wherever you are.

HEAVENLY HOME

The Lion's elegant style is often expressed through the beautiful decor or objets d'art and furniture that they choose for their home. To ensure that both you and your home are protected from negative energy, incorporate the following into your space. This simple ritual will keep your body (as well as your mind and spirit) in heavenly harmony, too.

You will need:
* 1 tiger's eye
* 1 sunstone
* 1 black tourmaline
* 1 red carnelian
* 1 citrine
* 1 blue lace agate
* 1 malachite
* A sandalwood incense stick

1. Place the tiger's eye in the south corner of your home, the sunstone to the north, the black tourmaline to the west, the red carnelian to the east.

2. Take the citrine, blue lace agate and malachite and group them together in a central spot in your home (perhaps in a tiny bowl).

3. Light the incense, then, holding the stick, walk around every space in your home to clear any negative energy and purify your sanctuary.

The complete crystal 'grid' you've created here contains all the energies needed to protect all those who live in your home; the seven stones are infused with a balance of energy to protect and enhance wellbeing throughout it.

WHEREVER YOU GO

Now if you're one of those highly social Lions, you probably spend more time out and about than in your sanctuary. You are bound to have a wide choice of exquisite jewellery, tasteful accessories and so on – and remember, you need to 'shine' brighter than anyone else, so be sure to flaunt it. However, twirling and flouncing about at social occasions and in the corridors of power are all well and good, but there are some who may cast negative psychic energy upon you, such as envy or scorn. So you also need to protect yourself out there in the big, wide world that you love so much.

You will need:
* A length of fine gold thread
* A plain gold band

1. Take the gold thread and wind it around and around the ring.

2. Tie the ends together.

3. Hold your talisman up to the sun (but don't look at the sun!) and say, 'With this golden band, I will be true to my solar nature, to shine without being tarnished by the darkness of others'.

Take your talisman with you wherever you go, to protect you from negativity, back-biting or envy from others, and to promote and reinforce your showy, fun-loving, magnanimous spirit.

WALK BAREFOOT

You probably have a fabulous collection of stylish shoes, but strutting one's stuff, or walking the walk, is about the beneficial contact of being in touch – literally – with Mother Earth.

Whenever you have a chance (obviously this is more do-able in warm weather), throw off those heels, sandals or boots and wiggle your toes in the sand, walk barefoot across dew-covered grass, plunge your feet into a cool stream or a gentle surf or march across the sun-baked earth, and experience the exchange of energy that flows between the soles of your feet and the planet.

SUN SALUTATION

Whether you're a courageous 'brave-heart' Leo, or a soft-hearted pussycat, this will set you up for the day ahead and honour the sun, your ruling planet. This is best done first thing in the morning, regardless of how lazy or (un)motivated you're feeling, and outside, for maximum exposure to the sun.

1. Relax, and stand straight with your arms by your sides, facing the direction of the sun (even if you can't see it).

2. Take two or three long in- and out-breaths, then raise your arms above your head and turn your palms to face each other.

3. Breathe slowly and deeply a few times, in and out, then sweep your arms around to meet in prayer in front of your chest. Hold again for a few deep breaths.

4. Raise your arms above your head as before.

5. Repeat five times, and you will feel revitalised and connected to the solar light within.

The sun salutation also reflects the light of the solar centre inside you, so welcome it into your life every day.

PART THREE

Caring For Your Soul

*Art washes away from the soul
the dust of everyday life.*

Pablo Picasso, painter

This final section offers you tailored, fun, easy and amazing ways to connect to and care for your sacred self. This, in turn, means you will begin to feel at one with the joyous energy of the Universe. You don't have to sign up to any religion or belief system (unless you want to) – just take some time to experience uplifting moments through your interaction with the spiritual aspects of the cosmos. Care for your sun sign's soul centre, and you care about the Universe, too.

The creative urge is a powerful impulse in the Leo psyche. In fact, creativity and its expression is one of the greatest ways to support your spiritual journey. Expressing what brings you joy and manifesting the imaginings of the mind and the feeling of something deeper at work within you as you do so is food for your soul.

All great artists, musicians and performers are informed by something divine that 'speaks' to them, whether a literal voice, an instinct or a feeling of being taken out of themselves and becoming one with the Universe. Whatever this 'feeling' or moment is, it generates the urge to create. (The word 'create' is rooted in a Latin word, meaning to 'bring into being'.)

Connecting to your sacred self may seem quite natural if you're already a highly creative and expressive Lion. But there are some Leos who, due to cultural or family expectations, may feel disconnected from this inner self. If you're not already developing or expressing your innate creative streak, now is the time to get on to it and begin to connect more closely to this mystery within you.

A YOGA CRYSTAL GRID

Leo's love of body movement means yoga and Pilates connect them to their unique creative spiritual energy. When you practise yoga, surround your mat or the room with a grid of crystals to energise, restore and balance you.

You will need:
* 4 sunstones
* 1 clear quartz crystal

1. Place one sunstone in the north of your practice space, one to the south, one to the east and one to the west (but not so close to you that you'll knock them by accident).

2. Before starting your yoga session, sit cross-legged and hold the clear quartz crystal close to your chest with both hands.

3. Focus for a moment on the balance of mind, body and spirit, then place the crystal alongside the sunstone at the head end of your mat or space.

4. Now go ahead with your session, aware that you are surrounded by empowering sunstone energy to promote and reinforce your physical wellbeing and Leonine self-empowerment.

....

KNOW YOUR AURA

It's hardly surprising that Leo drama queens and divas feel simply the best when wearing vibrant colours. But do you know what 'colour' your aura is radiating all around you? And, well, what is an aura anyway?

Briefly, universal energy flows through all things, and when it exudes from the physical body it is known as the 'aura'. Our state of being or mood at any given time 'colours' the pure energy of the Universe radiating through us. Like the colours of the rainbow, the aura sets your own personality barcode, revealing specific qualities or moods that you are expressing.

Try this simple exercise to see which colour is the most dominant in your aura at any moment in time and which of the crystals to focus on for a deeper connection to the invisible force that flows through you.

Below is a checklist of seven basic colours of the aura, plus white or no colour, to represent the pure energy of the Universe. Decide which *one word* connects most to your feelings and mood right now (they are all words associated with your Leo personality). Even if you opt for a slightly negative word, by aligning yourself to the right crystal you will be empowered and inspired and any negative feelings will disappear. Don't cheat and choose *a colour*; just pick *a word* from the following list:

* Red – fiery, dramatic, inspirational, challenging, angry (red carnelian)
* Orange – friendly, playful, impressive, optimistic, pessimistic (amber)
* Yellow – cheeky, adaptable, jovial, chatty, bored (citrine)
* Green – calm, unflappable, confident, unsure (malachite)
* Blue – serene, compassionate, calm, nurturing, confused (blue calcite)
* Indigo – wise, creative, idealistic, unproductive (lapis lazuli)
* Violet – imaginative, dreamy, escapist, lethargic (amethyst)
* White/crystal clear – empowered, self-reliant, connected to Nature, incompetent (clear quartz)

Place the appropriate crystal beside your bed or on your desk or carry it with you for twenty-four hours to deepen and boost your connection to the universal energy flow and to feel empowered. Repeat the exercise from time to time, to see if your aura energy flow has changed.

....

WINDOWS OF OPPPRTUNITY

Which part of the day gives you as a Leo most meaning, or happiness? Find this 'window of time' and use it to enhance your talents, show off your flamboyant nature to its best, push for business success or seal intentions to send off to the Universe to help you achieve your goals.

You will need:
* A pen and paper

1. Jot down a list throughout the day of 'how I spend my time'. It doesn't have to be very detailed, it could just be, for example: '8 a.m. breakfast', 'Went to work' and so on.

2. At the end of the day, observe your own handwriting: does it appear that at certain times your writing is more fluid, less rigid, more excited? Make a note of which time of day reflects more joy than others.

3. Now spend another day observing Nature and the weather: go for a walk, tend to the garden, be mindful of how you feel at different times. If you can see the sun, wonder at its power, and make a note of whether you preferred its colours and influence on the landscape at midday or at sunset and so on. Add these preferences to the list you wrote in Step 1, using the same time slots.

By identifying when in the day you find the most joy, you'll discover the part of the day that has the most spiritual meaning for you. You can then use this important time to maximise your affinity for the Universe, Nature, creativity and your sacred self.

A SHARE IN THE UNIVERSE

In keeping with the notion of good karma, by being the best of your Leo self, and giving of this self freely, you will reap the rewards of happiness, too.

One of the most gratifying and heart-warming things you can do is to teach someone one of your skills. Identify a skill and take double pleasure in performing it and passing it on, even if just by example. It could be anything from the way you act a role or bake a cake to creating a showcase interior or painting a masterpiece.

Affirm to yourself in quiet moments:

> My creativity and talent are not mine alone;
> they come from a divine source. I offer these
> talents freely, and I am happy to see others take
> pleasure and become the best of themselves,
> too.

Showing that you genuinely care about others by sharing your divine gifts will boost your own creative connection to the universal energy, while helping you to discover a sense of spiritual happiness.

....

THE SPIRIT OF CRYSTALS

Crystals have a mysterious power of their own, and if we start to love them and treat them as our friends, their energies can help us to enjoy being who we are. Labradorite embodies all of Leo's glitter, power, glory and dazzling spirit. So try this little ritual whenever you need a boost of spiritual power to show you the way.

You will need:
* A photo of yourself
* A mirror
* A piece of labradorite (this is a highly iridescent stone, so choose one that 'dances' before your eyes)
* A gold ribbon

1. Place the photo of yourself on a table in front of the mirror and gaze at your reflection while holding the labradorite.

2. Say, 'This beauty is my beauty, and this crystal will bring me esoteric knowledge and the mysteries of the soul'.

3. Place the crystal on the photo, then wind the gold ribbon around both of them to surround your 'petition'.

Leave overnight to charge the crystal with lunar and solar energy, then move the labradorite to a special place – say, a box or pouch – for future use.

Take up the crystal whenever you're in need of support, a sign or a message from (or a connection with) the Universe.

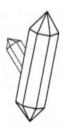

TIME OUT

Gregarious and at the centre of most social attention, there are times when even Leo needs to be alone to recharge. Use this visualisation to relax and invest in the joy of being at one with you, and to discover your sacred self.

1. Sit cross-legged and rest your hands on your knees.

2. Become aware of your breathing and take some long, deep breaths, in and out, until you find a relaxing rhythm.

3. Imagine a sunset: the light begins to alter, as the sun sets behind some distant hills, and the colours change – first to pinks, golds, oranges, then to shades of red and purple. You may even see the world transform like a prism, as green flashes of light – optical phenomena in the atmosphere – create a magical vista before your eyes.

4. Now imagine you are one of the Hesperides (the nymphs responsible for the light at sunset): you dance along the last rays of the sun and, as it begins to set above the horizon, you kiss the landscape, turning every tree golden, every meadow shades of orange and yellow. Then you dance away into the distant sky with the other nymphs as the sun disappears beneath the horizon. As you do so, take one last look at planet Earth, and know you are there to shine your light on the world; you are part of the Universe, not separate from it.

As you come out of your visualisation, you will feel at one with your sacred self.

Last Words

Being Leo is said to be a privilege, simply because your ruler, the sun, is not only the life-giving force of the solar system but is at the very heart of astrology. Being ruled by the sun puts you centre stage; you can't hide your light – you have to let it shine brightly and illuminate the world.

This kind of privilege means you have to live up to it, too. It can be hard work shining brightly everywhere you go. It can feel a struggle at times to push for the acclaim you deserve when you'd rather just go and scribble or paint. Yet if you care about you, nurturing and nourishing your amazing talents and taking pride in your beautiful personality, then privilege becomes a divine gift, and one that can lead you on to greater achievements by being true to your self.

This book has shown you how to care for and support your magnificent sense of purpose – how to inspire that fiery Leo creativity, cherish your feelings and enhance your love life. It has helped you to establish a respectful relationship with your body and to keep it beautiful. And, through your fiery vision and creative impulse, you have also discovered a spiritual connection, where you can nurture the sacredness inside you.

Whether you dance with your reflection in the mirror, embellish your body with divine products or simply paint a canvas from the soul, you shine your best when loving who you are. The authentic you is precious – so be true to your Leo potentials, and you'll find the greatest joy and happiness in becoming yourself.

Resources

Main sites for crystals, stones, candles, smudging sticks, incense, pouches, essential oils and everything needed for the holistic self-care practices included in this book:

holisticshop.co.uk
thepsychictree.co.uk
thesoulangels.co.uk
earthcrystals.com
livrocks.com
artisanaromatics.com

For a substantial range of books (and metaphysical items) on astrology, divination, runes, palmistry, tarot and holistic health, etc.:

thelondonastrologyshop.com
watkinsbooks.com
mysteries.co.uk
barnesandnoble.com
innertraditions.com

For more information on astrology, personal horo-scopes and birth-chart calculations:
astro-charts.com (simplest, very user friendly)

horoscopes.astro-seek.com
(straightforward)
astrolibrary.org/free-birth-chart
(easy to use, with lots of extra information)

Glossary

Aura An invisible electromagnetic energy field that emanates from and surrounds all living beings

Auric power The dominant colour of the aura, which reveals your current mood or state

Chakra Sanskrit for 'wheel', in Eastern spiritual traditions the seven chakras are the main epicentres – or wheels – of invisible energy throughout the body

Dark of the moon This is when the moon is invisible to us, due to its proximity to the sun; it is a time for reflection, solitude and a deeper awareness of oneself

Divination Gaining insight into the past, present and future using symbolic or esoteric means

Double-terminator crystal A quartz crystal with a point at each end, allowing its energy to flow both ways

Full moon The sun is at its maximum opposition to the moon, thus casting light across all of the moon's orb; in esoteric terms, it is a time for culmination, finalising deals, committing to love and so on

Geopathic stress Negative energy emanating from and on the Earth, such as underground water courses, tunnels, overhead electrical cables and geological faults

Grid A specific pattern or layout of items symbolising specific intentions or desires

Horoscope An astrological chart or diagram showing the position of the sun, moon and planets at the time of any given event, such as the moment of somebody's birth, a marriage or the creation of an enterprise; it is used to interpret the characteristics or to forecast the future of that person or event

New crescent moon A fine sliver of crescent light that appears curving outwards to the right in the northern hemisphere and to the left in the southern hemisphere; this phase is for beginning new projects, new romance, ideas and so on

Psychic energy One's intuition, sixth sense or instincts, as well as the divine, numinous or magical power that flows through everything

Shadow side In astrology, your shadow side describes those aspects of your personality associated with your opposite sign and of which you are not usually aware

Smudging Clearing negative energy from the home with a smouldering bunch of dried herbs, such as sage

Solar return salutation A way to give thanks and welcome the sun's return to your zodiac sign once a year (your birthday month)

Sun in opposition The sun as it moves through the opposite sign to your own sun sign

Sun sign The zodiac sign through which the sun was moving at the exact moment of your birth

Waning moon The phase of the moon after it is full, when it begins to lose its luminosity – the waning moon is illuminated on its left side in the northern hemisphere, and on its right side in the southern hemisphere; this is a time for letting go, acceptance and preparing to start again

Waxing moon The phase between a new and a full moon, when it grows in luminosity – the waxing moon is illuminated on its right side in the northern hemisphere and on its left side in the southern hemisphere; this is a time for putting ideas and desires into practice

Zodiac The band of sky divided into twelve segments (known as the astrological signs), along which the paths of the sun, the moon and the planets appear to move

About the Author

After studying at the Faculty of Astrological Studies in London, the UK, Sarah gained the Diploma in Psychological Astrology – an in-depth 3-year professional training programme cross-fertilised by the fields of astrology and depth, humanistic and transpersonal psychology. She has worked extensively in the media as astrologer for titles such as *Cosmopolitan* magazine (UK), *SHE, Spirit & Destiny* and the *London Evening Standard*, and appeared on UK TV and radio shows, including *Steve Wright in the Afternoon* on BBC Radio 2.

Her mainstream mind-body-spirit books include the international bestsellers, *The Tarot Bible, The Little Book of Practical Magic* and *Secrets of the Universe in 100 Symbols*.

Sarah currently practises and teaches astrology and other esoteric arts in the heart of the countryside.

Acknowledgements

I would first like to thank everyone at Yellow Kite, Hodder & Stoughton and Hachette UK who were part of the process of creating this series of twelve zodiac self-care books. I am especially grateful to Carolyn Thorne for the opportunity to write these guides; Anne Newman for her editorial advice, which kept me 'carefully' on the right track; and Olivia Nightingall who kept me on target for everything else! It is when people come together with their different skills and talents that the best books are made – so I am truly grateful for being part of this team.

See the full Astrology Self-Care series here

9781399704885   9781399704915   9781399704588

9781399704618   9781399704649   9781399704670

9781399704700   9781399704731   9781399704762

9781399704793   9781399704823   9781399704854

books to help you live a good life

Join the conversation and tell
us how you live a #goodlife

🐦 @yellowkitebooks
📘 YellowKiteBooks
📌 Yellow Kite Books
📷 YellowKiteBooks